TRANSIT AT THE TABLE III

A GUIDE TO EFFECTIVE
PARTICIPATION IN STATEWIDE
DECISIONMAKING FOR
TRANSIT AGENCIES IN NON-
URBANIZED AREAS

REPORT DOCUMENTATION PAGE

Form Approved
OMB No. 0704-0188

1. REPORT DATE (DD-MM-YYYY)	2. REPORT TYPE	3. DATES COVERED (From - To)
30-09-2011	Final Report	April 2008 - September 2011

4. TITLE AND SUBTITLE

Transit at the Table III: A Guide to Effective Participation in Statewide Decisionmaking for Transit Agencies in Non-Urbanized Areas

5a. CONTRACT NUMBER

5b. GRANT NUMBER

5c. PROGRAM ELEMENT NUMBER

6. AUTHOR(S)

William Lyons; Lindsey Morse; Benjamin Rasmussen

5d. PROJECT NUMBER

5e. TASK NUMBER

5f. WORK UNIT NUMBER

7. PERFORMING ORGANIZATION NAME(S) AND ADDRESS(ES)

Research and Innovative Technology Administration
John A. Volpe National Transportation Systems Center
55 Broadway
Cambridge, MA 02142

8. PERFORMING ORGANIZATION REPORT NUMBER

DOT-VNTSC-FTA-11-04

9. SPONSORING/MONITORING AGENCY NAME(S) AND ADDRESS(ES)

Federal Transit Administration
Office of Planning and Environment
1200 New Jersey Avenue SE
Washington, DC 20590

10. SPONSOR/MONITOR'S ACRONYM(S)

FTA TPE

11. SPONSOR/MONITOR'S REPORT NUMBER(S)

FTA MA-27-1013

12. DISTRIBUTION/AVAILABILITY STATEMENT

13. SUPPLEMENTARY NOTES

FTA Project Contact: P. John Sprowls, Community Planner, Federal Transit Administration
Phone: 202-366-5362; Fax: 202-493-2478; Email: john.sprowls@dot.gov

14. ABSTRACT

This report draws upon eight State case studies to identify processes, experiences, and results of transit participation in statewide planning with a focus on non-urbanized or rural areas. Transit at the Table III is intended as a resource for organizations directly or indirectly involved in providing rural transit – state DOTs, regional planning organizations (RPOs), rural transit agencies, and their partners, including business, universities, Tribes, federal land management units, health care providers, and others. This study is the third in the "Transit at the Table" series on successful participation by transit agencies in federally-required metropolitan area and statewide transportation planning processes. This report consists of a synthesis of the case studies, a discussion of observations and challenges, a section on the role of transit in rural livability, a self-assessment checklist for transit operators, and a list of resources. This report is a product of the Federal Transit Administration and Federal Highway Administration Transportation Planning Capacity Building Program and can be found at www.planning.dot.gov along with case studies of each of the eight States.

15. SUBJECT TERMS

Keywords: transit, statewide planning, rural planning, regional planning

16. SECURITY CLASSIFICATION OF:			17. LIMITATION OF ABSTRACT	18. NUMBER OF PAGES	19a. NAME OF RESPONSIBLE PERSON
a. REPORT	b. ABSTRACT	c. THIS PAGE			P. John Sprowls, FTA
N/A	N/A	N/A	None.	43	19b. TELEPHONE NUMBER (Include area code) 202-366-5362

Reset

Standard Form 298 (Rev. 8/98)
Prescribed by ANSI Std. Z39.18

Acknowledgments

Throughout the study, Technical Working Group (TWG) members provided valuable insight and advice to the Federal Transit Administration (FTA) and the study team. A complete list of TWG membership may be found below. The study team also wants to acknowledge the participants in the study: the State Departments of Transportation (SDOTs), rural or regional planning organizations (RPOs), rural transit agencies, and other entities. A complete list of the States and agencies that participated may be found in Appendix C: Non-SDOT Study Participants.

Research Study Team

William Lyons, Project Manager
Community Planner, John A. Volpe National Transportation Systems Center

Lindsey Morse
Community Planner, John A. Volpe National Transportation Systems Center

Benjamin Rasmussen
Community Planner, John A. Volpe National Transportation Systems Center

Federal Transit Administration

Charlie Goodman, P. John Sprowls, Chanel Winston, Candace Noonan, Lorna Wilson, Joanne Waszczak, David Schneider

Federal Highway Administration

Susan Grosser

Technical Working Group

- Fred Abousleman, Executive Director, National Association of Regional Councils
- Brian Alberts, Multi-State Technical Assistance Program Coordinator, American Association of State Highway and Transportation Officials*
- Ed Beimborn, Former Chair, Transportation Research Board (TRB) Public Transportation Planning and Development Committee (AP025) / Professor Emeritus, University of Wisconsin-Milwaukee
- Matt Chase, Executive Director, National Association of Development Organizations
- Rod Clark, Director of Bureau of Transit, Local Roads, Railroads, and Harbors, Wisconsin Department of Transportation
- Priscilla Fraser, Executive Director, South Central Council of Governments
- Nicole Goldsmith, Executive Director, Rural Transit Assistance Program*
- Brendon Hemily, Chair, TRB Public Transportation Planning and Development Committee / Consultant
- Patricia Hendren, Chair, TRB Statewide Multimodal Transportation Planning Committee (ADA10) / Director, Office of Performance, Washington Metropolitan Area Transit Authority
- Steve Kish, State Transit Manager, Georgia Department of Transportation
- Carrie Kissel, Senior Program Manager, National Association of Development Organizations
- Michelle Maggiore, Program Director for Policy and Planning, American Association of State Highway and Transportation Officials*
- Keith Melton, Community Planner, Federal Transit Administration Region IV
- Elizabeth Orr, Community Planner, Federal Transit Administration Region IV
- Robert Padgette, Director of Policy Development and Outreach, American Association of State Highway and Transportation Officials*
- Diane Quigley, Transit Planning Administration, Florida Department of Transportation
- Leigh Ann Trainer, Transportation Services Unit Chief, Georgia Department of Human Resources
- Richard Weaver, Director, Planning, Policy, and Sustainability, American Public Transportation Association
- Erika Young, Transportation Director, National Association of Regional Councils
- Chris Zeilinger, Director, National Resource Center for Human Service Transportation Coordination, Community Transit Association of America

---

* No longer with the organization

TRANSIT AT THE TABLE III

Table of Contents

Verde Valley Transit Facility – Arizona
Photograph provided by Northern Arizona Intergovernmental Public Transportation Authority

Chapter 1:
Introduction

Transit at the Table III: A Guide to Effective Participation in Statewide Decisionmaking for Transit Agencies in Non-Urbanized Areas examines successful approaches to considering rural transit in statewide transportation planning. It uses eight State case studies to identify processes, experiences, and results of transit agency participation in statewide transportation planning, focusing on non-urbanized or rural areas. This report consists of the following sections:

- Synthesis;
- Observations and Challenges;
- The Role of Transit in Rural Livability;
- A Self-Assessment Checklist for Transit Operators;
- Resources and References; and
- Non-SDOT Study Participants.

In addition, separate and detailed case studies of each of the eight States are available online on the Federal Transit Administration (FTA) and Federal Highway Administration (FHWA) Transportation Planning Capacity Building website (http://www.planning.dot.gov/).

This study was conducted for the FTA Office of Planning and the Environment by the U.S. Department of Transportation's John A. Volpe National Transportation Systems Center.

1.1 Purpose and Audience

Transit at the Table III examines the full range of activities conducted as part of statewide transportation planning processes, from use of vision plans; setting goals, policies, and priorities; establishing performance measures; involving stakeholders and the public; selecting investments; and implementing projects. The research study recognizes that statewide planning, and participating agencies and partners, vary in each State and that variation has implications for how rural transit considerations are reflected in these processes. This study evaluates how and when these considerations are incorporated within statewide transportation planning, whether through policies, programs, technical processes, or collaboration and partnerships.

This study's major contribution will be to provide examples of effective approaches that will assist peer rural transit and regional planning agencies to work more effectively with State Departments of Transportation (SDOTs) to ensure that transit is considered in statewide planning and decisionmaking. Statewide planning guides important transportation resource allocation decisions that play a major role in the life of residents of rural areas — from meeting basic mobility and accessibility needs to supporting economic development and provision of health and human services. This report includes a detailed section examining the role transit, supported by statewide transportation planning, can play in improving the livability of rural communities. This topic reflects top priorities of the Secretary of the U.S. Department of Transportation and FTA and is related to the DOT-HUD-EPA Partnership for Sustainable Communities.

This report will provide a resource for organizations directly or indirectly involved in planning for and providing rural transit — SDOTs, regional or rural planning organizations (to be referred to as RPOs), rural transit providers and their partners, including businesses, universities, Tribes, Federal land management units, health care providers, and others. This study is intended to improve the effectiveness of transit participation in statewide transportation planning, the multimodal content of statewide transportation plans and programs, and ultimately, the delivery of transit services.

1.2 Transit at the Table Series

This report is the third in the Transit at the Table series on successful consideration of transit in the transportation planning process. The first study, completed in 2004, focused on participation by transit agencies in Metropolitan Planning Organizations (MPOs) in large urbanized areas, defined as those areas with populations greater than 200,000. The second study, completed in 2010, provided insights into participation by transit agencies in MPOs in small urbanized areas, defined as those areas with populations between 50,000 and 200,000. The covers of the first two studies are shown in Figure 1.

Recognizing that transportation needs and planning issues differ between urban, rural, or non-urbanized areas, this report identifies both the similarities and the unique aspects associated with these areas. In Transit at the Table I and II, the main participants in the planning processes of interest, and their roles and responsibilities, are clearly identifiable. Both of the earlier studies focused on close collaboration between MPOs and transit agencies, with support from the SDOT and other entities. Although some relevant aspects of the planning roles played by SDOTs and rural transit agencies are defined by Federal regulations and programs, the interaction between the two and the participation of other entities varies greatly among the States studied. Figure 2 summarizes the contrast between the clear roles of planning agencies studied in Transit at the

Figure 1. Covers of Transit at the Table I and II

Large urbanized areas (population greater than 200,000)

Small- and medium-sized urbanized areas (population between 50,000 and 200,000)

Figure 2. Comparison of Transit at the Table I and II Participants and Transit at the Table III Participants

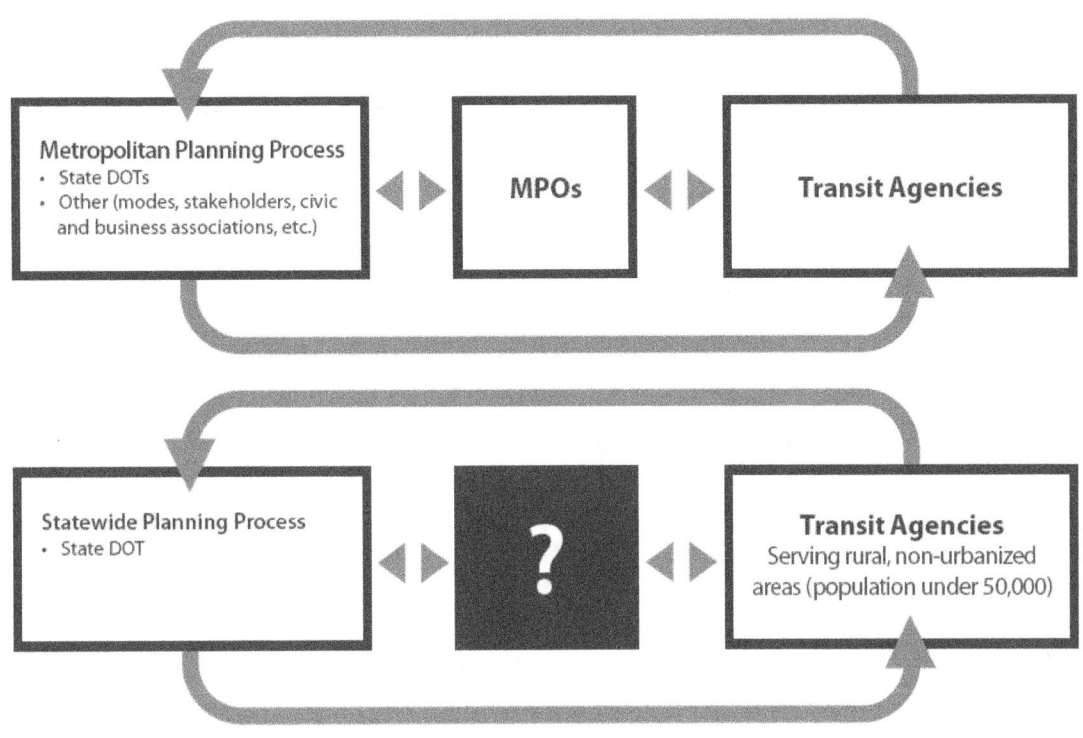

Table I and II and the less clear and more broadly ranging roles identified in Transit at the Table III.

1.3 Methodology

This report is based on structured discussions with staff and officials from eight SDOTs, over 20 RPOs, and over 20 rural transit providers, either local government or non-profits, as well as from several other State agencies, and transit associations. A Technical Working Group (TWG) assisted the study team in identifying key topics of interest and in selecting case study States. The TWG included representatives from the American Public Transportation Association (APTA), Association

of American State Highway and Transportation Officers (AASHTO), Community Transportation Association of America (CTAA), National Association of Development Organizations (NADO), National Association of Regional Councils (NARC), and the Transportation Research Board (TRB) Statewide Multimodal Transportation and Public Transportation Planning and Development Committees. In addition to the TWG, the study team conducted discussions with key stakeholders at the NARC 43rd Annual Conference and Exhibition on June 2, 2009, in Denver, CO, and at the National Rural Transportation Peer Learning Conference in

Figure 3. Map of Case Study States for Transit at the Table III

October 2009 and October 2010. These discussions helped inform the study by providing and then confirming common themes and issues.

The study team selected eight States based on input from FTA and the TWG, with consideration of geographic location, prevalence of rural transit, presence of public lands units and Tribes, and perception of successful planning processes. The study recognizes there are other States that would also serve as good case studies; FTA hopes to continue to research and highlight these examples in the future. Within each State, the team held three structured discussions with State, regional, and local participants that were chosen based on similar criteria, with input from the SDOT.

The eight States highlighted in the study are listed below and shown in Figure 3:

- Arizona
- Georgia
- Iowa
- Maine
- Minnesota
- Pennsylvania
- South Carolina
- Washington

1.4 Structure

As noted above, this report consists of sections on: synthesis; observations and challenges; the role of transit in rural livability; a self-assessment checklist for transit operators; and resources and references. In addition, eight separate State case studies are available online at the FTA/FHWA Transportation Planning Capacity Building website.

The first section identifies five attributes of planning identified by the study team as important to successful integration of rural transit in statewide planning: goals, planning products and processes, institutional relationships, funding, and service. The team placed each planning attribute along a continuum to describe an evolution from basic to more complete or thorough approaches. The study team used this continuum as a framework to describe and assess approaches to statewide planning and rural transit in each of the States studied. The team also used the framework to highlight examples of how different States effectively consider rural transit in statewide planning.

The observations and challenges section highlights those findings that were not captured in the continuum because of their cross-cutting nature and important and timely relevance to the national context. These include success in the context of limited and constrained resources; changing perceptions of rural transit; performance measures; and Tribal transit.

The role of transit in rural livability section presents observations and insights into how statewide transportation planning can strengthen the role transit plays in creating livable rural communities.

It draws both from the framework presented in the findings section as well as the Livability Principles of the DOT-HUD-EPA Partnership for Sustainable Communities and other resources, and is based on the Transit at the Table III case studies and synthesis.

The self-assessment checklist for transit operators presents a series of questions that SDOTs, RPOs, rural transit providers, and others can use to assess rural transit participation in statewide planning. The checklist is intended to facilitate discussion among planning partners on how to improve their collaboration and delivery of transportation services.

The eight case studies identify the service characteristics, institutional structure, and funding of rural transit in the assessment of how rural transit is incorporated within statewide planning, including interactions between entities, major planning and project initiatives, and observations and challenges.

Rainbow Rider vehicle and maintenance facility – Minnesota
Photograph provided by Rainbow Rider

Chapter 2: Synthesis

According to the research from Transit at the Table III, the extent and characteristics of rural transit participation in statewide transportation planning and decisionmaking vary by State and within each State. Such variation is a result of a number of contextual factors, from funding availability to the organizational structure of the SDOT. This section summarizes and organizes the main findings from the case studies by first introducing a continuum along which SDOTs, regions, and rural transit agencies involved in the study participate in statewide transportation planning as it relates to rural transit. The continuum is organized into five attributes of statewide transportation planning that are relevant to rural transit participation. The continuum is intended to assist peer agencies in interpreting and differentiating among the range of successful planning approaches the study team identified in each of the eight case studies, and to provide a sense of evolution from basic to more advanced approaches.

The rest of this section expands on the five attributes of the continuum to highlight successful and innovative approaches, interpret trends, and document challenges, with examples from the complete case studies, which are posted on the FTA and FHWA Transportation Planning Capacity Building website (http://www.planning.dot.gov/).

2.1 Continuum of Rural Transit Participation in Statewide Decisionmaking

The continuum presented in Table 1 is organized into five categories the study team identified as essential to successful integration of rural transit in statewide planning: goals, planning products and processes, institutional relationships, funding, and service. These categories and their order are intended to signify the statewide planning process for rural transit, from goal setting to implementation and delivery of services, which was found in Transit at the Table III. This section describes where along the continuum the States evaluated may lie and highlights examples of some successful approaches to achieving effective rural transit participation in statewide planning.

Table 1. Continuum of Rural Transit Participation in Statewide Decisionmaking

Category	Baseline (Basic Approach)	Advanced/Evolving Approach
Goals	Mobility and accessibility by transit	Livability and sustainability: economic development, equity, environment, multimodal and intermodal connections
Planning Products and Processes	State Long-Range Transportation Plan (LRTP), State Transportation Improvement Program (STIP), Human Services Coordinated Plan	State, regional, and local rural transit plan/studies, rural regional LRTPs and TIPs, Comprehensive Plan
Institutional Relationships	Limited interactions for funding and compliance between DOT and transit agency	Informal and formal collaboration, two-way communication, close relationships across multiple entities and jurisdictions
Funding	FTA programs	Other sources, including non-DOT, public and private
Service	Within jurisdiction only, human services and transit-dependent riders	Regional and intercity connections, human services, transit-dependent, and choice riders

2.2 Goals

Setting goals is the first step in the planning process. For statewide planning, goals are defined in the statewide long-range transportation plan (LRTP) and other documents, but also articulated through State initiatives and funding programs. Although the State legislature and SDOT set State level goals, these are influenced both by Federal goals and initiatives and by local and regional concerns and priorities. While the goals themselves are critical, how the goals are selected, applied, and supported is also important. Statewide goals should guide rural transit service and planning, but rural transit goals should also be included in statewide planning and programs.

Mobility (movement of riders) and accessibility (access to key destinations) can be considered as "baseline" or most common or basic goals that are reflected in statewide planning for rural transit. Additional goals, less common and more complex, include livability and sustainability in terms of economic development, quality of life, social equity, or environmental quality (e.g., air quality or climate change), and multimodal and intermodal connections. Most of the case study States demonstrate these advanced goals in the statewide planning processes that include rural transit. Common goals for this context are economic development, environment, and quality of life, which are addressed together because of their interdependence.

Economic Development

Both Maine and Pennsylvania place strong emphasis on economic development, possibly because their RPOs are either combined with, or based on, State economic development districts (EDDs). EDDs are designated by the Department of Commerce's Economic Development Administration (EDA). One of the primary activities of the EDDs is to work with an extensive network of public and private stakeholders to develop Comprehensive Economic Development Strategies (CEDS). Projects included

in the CEDS document or consistent with it may be eligible for EDA funding and, where job creation is an anticipated benefit, may be paired with funds from other Federal agencies, like U.S. DOT. Consequently, the activities that RPOs conduct for economic development naturally extend to include related issues like land use, transportation, housing, and workforce development.

Maine's statewide LRTP, Connecting Maine (2008),[1] focuses on integrating land use, transportation, and economic development, although it also considers sustainability. The plan's framework consists of 38 Corridors of Regional Economic Significance for Transportation focused on multimodal intercity connections, but many of the cities are classified as rural or the corridors pass through rural areas. In addition to this State and regional effort, economic development is a recognized local goal and priority associated with transit, as demonstrated by support for and success of Island Explorer bus systems that serve tourism areas.

Pennsylvania took a similar approach in its Land Use, Transportation, and Economic Development (LUTED) Initiative, which consisted of statewide and regional conferences at which specific objectives and action steps were identified. Although further State and Federal coordination has been limited, several RPOs recognized the potential for such coordination and have acted at the regional level to coordinate funding applications and projects. For example, some RPOs have incorporated their LUTED plan with their LRTP and CEDS. The coordination of these plans has allowed the RPOs to access different funding sources and to take a more comprehensive approach to planning and programming projects.

Economic development is also a transportation planning priority for Georgia, as outlined in its

---

1   http://www.maine.gov/mdot/connectingmaine/index.htm

State LRTP. This is also the case for South Carolina, where there is an ongoing statewide transit return on investment study and a requirement for Statewide Transportation Improvement Program (STIP) projects to be evaluated for economic development potential. At the local level, rural transit and intercity services are regarded as essential in getting people to work. In South Carolina, transit providers report successful partnerships with developers, universities, and businesses aimed at maintaining and growing the local economy. As one South Carolina transit agency noted, "economic development is at the table" and "getting people to work is very important."

Environment

In terms of the environment, climate change and sustainability goals are reflected in many of the case study State transportation plans and environmental initiatives; strategies to achieve reduced greenhouse gas (GHG) emissions and improved energy efficiency are also showing success at the local transit agency level in several States. Although some rural transit agencies identified climate change and air quality as urban issues, most feel that rural transit has a role to play in protecting the environment and supporting sustainable practices. Several SDOTs, such as Washington State DOT (WSDOT), recognize that sustainability and climate change performance measures, such as vehicle miles traveled (VMT), have different significance for rural compared to urban areas, but that environmental goals are relevant for all communities. Participants also pointed out that many rural communities are interested in preserving the natural beauty of their environment for both quality of life and economic development.

At the State level, the Maine Climate Action Plan (http://www.maine.gov/dep/air/greenhouse/), developed from the Maine Greenhouse Gas Initiative, recommends increasing "the availability of low-GHG

travel choices, such as transit (rail and bus), vanpools, walking, and biking" as well as "complementary land-use and location efficiency policies, and transit-based incentives to improve the attractiveness of low-GHG travel choices" and lists transit ridership as a potential performance measure. In Washington, WSDOT requires all State grant recipients to have sustainability plans and has long-standing and successful Transportation Demand Management and Commute Trip Reduction programs.

At the regional levels, some RPOs play a valuable role in sustainability and other initiatives because of their organization's multiple purposes, including transportation, community and economic development, and land use. Other RPOs without this broad functionality reported limitations to their ability to effectively manage issues such as jobs-housing balance. At the local level, bus replacement requests for alternative fueled vehicles and for downsizing to smaller vehicles and incorporation of "green" elements into facilities – such as geothermal and solar – are becoming more common. Several agencies took advantage of the recent American Recovery and Reinvestment Act (ARRA) funding, including the Transit Investments for Greenhouse Gas and Energy Reduction (TIGGER) grants, to request such capital investments. Rural transit agencies and RPOs are also using Congestion Mitigation and Air Quality (CMAQ) Improvement Program funds for a number of projects (see next section).

Quality of Life

According to several rural transit agencies, the public is beginning to see the value in transit for their everyday lives, as indicated already in association with economic development and environment. In Georgia, Coweta County attributes its ability to start a local demand response service and interest in a fixed-route system transit service to the community's positive reception of a Georgia Regional Transportation Authority

(GRTA) commuter bus to Atlanta, an example of evolution and expansion of rural transit. In South Carolina, RPOs and transit providers have seen a positive response to transit-related investments in marketing, education outreach, and innovative services such as a "Link to Lunch" high frequency circulator and Google transit trip planner.

2.3 Planning Processes and Products

The baseline requirement for rural transit participation in the development of plans, as identified in the above continuum, consists of local official consultation[2] for the statewide transportation plan; project inclusion in the STIP; and local development of a coordinated public transit-human service transportation plan as required for projects to be eligible for FTA Section 5310, 5316, and 5317 programs. More advanced planning practices include development of Transportation Improvement Programs (TIPs) and LRTPs for non-urbanized areas; statewide, regional, or local rural transit plans or other transit-focused studies; frequent consultation and technical assistance for a variety of plans and studies that bring in considerations from other sectors such as economic development or health; and substantive changes in the statewide transportation plan to include rural transit concerns and goals.

Regional Plans and Consultation

Some SDOTs hold their RPOs to the same or similar standards for comprehensive, coordinated, and continuous planning as for MPOs, while others rely on the RPOs for technical assistance and outreach support for the statewide plan. Thus, some of the case study SDOTs contract with or require RPOs to provide one, some, or all of the following: Unified or Rural Planning Work Programs (U/RPWPs), TIPs, LRTPs, coordinated plans, and/or other plans. In Georgia, the RPOs

conduct rural transit development plans with Georgia Department of Transportation (GDOT) funding. One RPO's plans include demographic projections, transit system characteristics, and a five-year forecast of operating and capital outlays. Whether the RPOs provide formal written plans or limit their contribution to outreach and assistance, SDOTs benefit from the regional perspective, which assists them to understand how needs differ significantly across the State.

Targeted State Programs

In addition to relying on RPOs to assist in planning and outreach with rural transit agencies, some SDOTs provide specific programs targeted at rural areas. Arizona DOT (ADOT) has a program, Planning Assistance for Rural Areas (PARA),[3] that provides FHWA planning and research funds to non-metropolitan communities to conduct multimodal transportation planning studies, which can include transit demand modeling and planning. Eligible applicants include counties, cities, and towns located outside the boundaries of Arizona's two Transportation Management Associations (TMAs), Phoenix and Tucson, as well as all Tribal governments. ADOT funds 100 percent of the study process. In 2009, it had $2 million available, which was distributed to 13 communities, seven of which explicitly addressed transit needs and opportunities in their studies.

Sustained Coordination

In some States, the coordinated plan provides opportunities for RPOs, SDOTs, MPOs, and rural agencies to build relationships and coordinate on other activities. In Pennsylvania, one RPO has successfully reconvened a group established to develop the region's human services coordinated plan. Known as the Coordinated Public Human Services Committee, the group meets twice a year including an annual application process meeting. The group provides a forum for transit operators

---

2 http://www.fhwa.dot.gov/planning/statewide/localoff.html

3 http://www.azdot.gov/mpd/systems_planning/PDF/PARA/PARAs.asp

to communicate about what they are doing, the services they are providing, and opportunities for coordination.

Statewide Plans

Case study States demonstrate success in both incorporating rural transit into statewide plans and engaging rural transit in the statewide plan development.

According to ADOT officials, both "Building a Quality Arizona (bqAZ)," a visionary process to develop a State transportation planning framework, and "What Moves You Arizona?," the update to the LRTP, are using an approach regarded as a "sea change" for Arizona because it includes transit, consolidates several regional plans, and "shifts how we do business — moving to multimodal planning from highway-focused planning."

Georgia's statewide transportation plan included two scenarios, which for rural transit translated into either maintaining the existing service (No Build) or expanding rural transit service to all rural counties at current per capita service level (Build). The forecasted financial and service needs of the plan influenced the design and passage of the Transportation Investment Act of 2010, which may provide a new resource for funding for transit. Other State plans, such as Pennsylvania's, are designed to be mode-neutral so rural transit is not explicitly addressed. However, it is significant that Pennsylvania did include rural transit in the process by ensuring its development team included representatives from rural transit and several organizations dependent on rural transit such as Area Agencies on Aging.

2.4 Institutional Relationships

The baseline relationship is for the SDOT to provide technical assistance, including on FTA grant applications, to rural transit agencies. Advanced relationships consist of participation by other players, including providers of planning, training, and additional services, as indicated by Figure 4. All of the case study States had some form of rural or regional transportation

Figure 4. Diagram of Interactions between the Statewide Planning Process and Rural Transit Agencies

Who is in the blackbox? What role do they play?
- Local governments and other local jurisdictions
- Statewide transit association, community transportation association, other associations
- Councils of Government, Regional Planning or Development Organizations
- Community-based human service transportation agencies and providers
- Regional Transportation Assistance Program Advisory Committee
- Tribal governments and Federal public land agencies

Table 2. Rural or Regional Planning Organization Information by State

State	RPO Name	Relationship with SDOT	Services Provided
Arizona	Councils of Government (COGs)	Overall Work Plan	TIP, coordinated plan, FTA/State application process
Georgia	Regional Commissions (RCs)	Legislatively created, SDOT planning contracts	Rural transit development plans
Iowa	Regional Planning Affiliations (RPAs)	SDOT designation, Transportation Planning Work Program	TIP, LRTP, coordinated plan, and public participation plan
Maine	Regional Planning Commissions (RPCs)	Biennial cooperative agreements	Events and outreach for statewide transportation plan, facilitate communication and technical assistance
Minnesota	Regional Development Commissions (RDCs) and Area Transportation Partnerships (ATPs)	Work Plan	Coordinated plan, TIP
Pennsylvania	Rural Planning Organizations (RPOs)	UPWP	TIP, LRTP, coordinated plan
South Carolina	Councils of Government (COGs)	Memorandum of Agreement (MOA) and RPWP	LRTP, outreach for State plan
Washington	Regional Transportation Planning Organizations (RTPOs) and Councils of Government (COGs)	Authorized by legislation but voluntary, SDOT contract	TIP, LRTP, coordinated plan

organizations (RPOs), although the term varies by State and sometimes involves two coordinating entities (see Table 2). RPOs are often housed within multi-purpose regional planning commissions or councils of governments (COGs) that have several State and Federal designations, such as the EDDs discussed under Goals. Regional transportation agencies or authorities (RTAs), a term which also varies by State, also play a significant role in some of the States and either function as or with the RPOs. Iowa and Maine have such entities designated statewide while Arizona, Georgia, and South Carolina have several pilot entities.

The case study States reflect a number of different models for successful interaction between SDOTs and rural transit agencies. Often, more than one model exists within a single State, creating both direct and indirect connections. These models include, but are not limited to, the five depicted in Figure 5. Note that in some cases, a transit agency may be housed in

an RPO. These models are not necessarily mutually exclusive for each State as they vary by the purpose of the interaction and also sometimes by the nature of the transit agency or RPO. In addition, some States do not have separate transit and planning SDOT offices; most that do, have high levels of coordination between the offices.

In addition to RPOs, other important entities include State transit associations, statewide coordination councils, other State agencies, MPOs, Tribes (which will be discussed later under Observations and Challenges), and Federal land management agencies, such as the National Park Service (NPS) (see discussion of the Acadia Island Explorer later in this section).

Each of the eight States has an active State transit association. At a minimum, these provide training, advocacy, or networking opportunities to members

Figure 5. Five Models of How Rural Transit Agencies Interact with the Statewide Planning Process

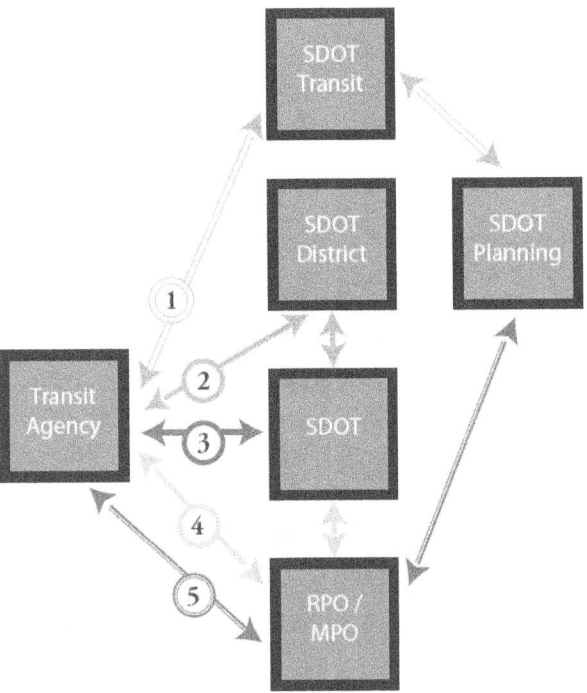

and at a maximum, provide all three services, are key partners with the SDOT, and represent and serve all transit agencies within the State, including rural. The following examples highlight some successful practices of transit associations in the case study States:

- PennDOT and rural transit operators credited the Pennsylvania Public Transportation Association with engaging rural transit providers and facilitating networking despite distances between rural transit agencies.

- All 35 transit agencies in Iowa belong to the Iowa Public Transit Association, which holds four meetings each year that are attended by Iowa DOT.

- The Georgia Transit Association provides a discounted membership rate for rural systems and has attracted the participation of the Human Services Transportation Subcommittee of the Georgia Association of Regional Commissions.

- The Arizona Transit Association has a close working relationship with ADOT, including ADOT representation on its Board of Directors and collaboration with ADOT to conduct the first statewide rural transit needs study.

Six (WA, SC, MN, IA, AZ, and GA) of the case study States noted the existence of statewide coordination councils. Nearly all of the councils were formed to coordinate human services and public transportation, but also address a number of broad transit considerations. Examples of the councils include:

- The mission of Washington's Agency Council on Coordinated Transportation (ACCT) is to promote and provide oversight for the coordination of special needs transportation, provide a forum for discussing issues and initiating change, and report to the legislature and propose legislative remedies. In 2010, ACCT membership included the head of WSDOT's Public Transportation Division, the head of Yakima Valley COG as the representative for all of the RTPOs, and representatives from schools, users of special needs transportation and the State Department of Social and Health Services.

- Georgia's new Coordinating Committee for Rural and Human Services Transportation will involve GDOT and the Department of Human Services as well as other agencies, and is required to consider strategies for vehicle sharing, route coordination, consolidation, funding restrictions, and cost reduction.

- The Iowa Transportation Coordination Council (ITCC) is intended to review institutional and regulatory transportation coordination issues and has produced a number of action plans. The latest plan is in draft form and includes sections on volunteer transportation, evaluation of the Medicaid brokerage, mobility management, and a strategy to "Engage, Educate, Energize."

- The South Carolina Interagency Transportation Coordination Council is intended to promote interagency and statewide cooperation in the provision and management of transportation programs and has been charged with identifying needs and constraints in terms of funding, operations, and other considerations.

Human service transportation coordination also leads to collaboration and coordination with the State's department of health and human services. Georgia demonstrates a relatively high level of coordination between GDOT and the Department of Human Services (DHS). The State has regional DOT and DHS transportation coordinators who provide a link between their State agencies and Regional Commissions (RCs) and transit agencies. DHS actually manages the FTA Section 5310 program and contracts with Section 5311 recipients to provide human service transportation.

2.5 Funding Sources and Strategies

Baseline funding for rural transit consists of fares and funding from FTA Section 5311 Formula Grants for Other than Urbanized Areas. Advanced funding consists of additional FTA grant programs, FHWA flex and planning funds, SDOT transit funding, other State agency funding, and other local strategies.

U.S. DOT Funding

FTA has a number of grant programs that are relevant to rural transit. These primarily consist of the following, which can be found on the FTA Grant Programs webpage (http://www.fta.dot.gov/funding/grants_financing_263.html):

- Section 5304: Statewide Planning

- Section 5305: Planning Programs

- Section 5310 Transportation for Elderly Persons and Persons with Disabilities

- Section 5311 Formula Grants for Other than Urbanized Areas

  - 5311(b)(3) – Rural Transit Assistance Program (RTAP)

  - 5311(c) – Public Transportation on Indian Reservations (Tribal Transit Program)[4]

  - 5311(f) – Intercity Bus Program

- Section 5316 Job Access and Reverse Commute (JARC) Program

- Section 5317 New Freedom (NF)

- Section 5320 Paul S. Sarbanes Transit in Parks (TRIP) Program (formerly Alternative Transportation in Parks and Public Lands (ATPPL) Program)

Several participants commented favorably on the Section 5316 (Job Access and Reverse Commute) and 5317 (New Freedom) programs. In Arizona, participants report a sense that those programs emerged in response to State and local needs communicated nationally and that such programs, when combined with Section 5310 and Section 5311 programs, have the potential to provide more cost-efficient and extensive service.

In addition to these grants, a number of other FTA discretionary grant programs provide funding to rural transit, including those under the

---

4 The primary source of transportation funding for Indian Tribes is through the Indian Reservation Roads (IRR) program, which is jointly administered by Federal Highway Administration's Office of Federal Lands Highway and the Department of Interior's Bureau of Indian Affairs IRR is supposed to consider transit but does not have enough funding for transit to compete with roads and bridges SAFETEA-LU created a new FTA program, the Tribal Transit Program (TTP) (49 U S C 5311(c)), which makes funds available to Federally-recognized Indian Tribes or Alaska Native villages, groups, or communities as identified by the Bureau of Indian Affairs (BIA) in the U S Department of the Interior for public transportation capital projects, operating costs, and planning activities that are eligible costs under the FTA Section 5311 Non-Urbanized Area Formula Program No cost sharing is required for this program; the Federal grant may fund up to 100 percent of eligible project costs However, FTA encourages Tribes to leverage the program funds and demonstrate local commitment through in-kind contributions and use of other funding sources that are available to support public transportation service

ARRA, in particular the Transportation Investment Generating Economic Recovery (TIGER)[5] and TIGGER[6] grants. Other U.S. DOT programs used for rural transit funding include the Surface Transportation Program (STP), State Planning and Research (SPR) Program, and the CMAQ Improvement Program.

The STP[7] provides flexible funding that may be used by States and localities for projects on any Federal-aid highway, including the National Highway System, bridge projects on any public road, transit capital projects, and intracity and intercity bus terminals and facilities. Case study participants reported varying levels of flexible funding use. For example, for FY09, Arizona flexed over 20 percent of its $6.5 million in STP flex funding to Section 5310 projects and allocated the remainder to Sections 5311 and 5307 (Urbanized Area Formula Program) recipients based on population.

The SPR[8] Program is a result of a requirement by SAFETEA-LU that States set aside 2 percent of the apportionments they receive from the Interstate Maintenance, National Highway System, Surface Transportation, Highway Bridge, CMAQ Improvement Program,[9] and Equity Bonus programs for State planning and research activities. South Carolina and Iowa SDOTs reported using SPR to fund planning studies and other activities by the RPOs or equivalents.

The CMAQ Improvement Program is jointly administered by FHWA and FTA. These agencies fund projects that improve air quality and reduce congestion in nonattainment areas, or those areas that have been determined not to meet the National Ambient Air Quality Standards for ozone, carbon monoxide, and particulate matter. CMAQ funds are often used to improve the efficiency of motor vehicle traffic by investing in incident response and congestion improvements, but transit and nonmotorized investments are also eligible. MaineDOT has taken advantage of CMAQ funds to support three-year start-up periods for the Island Explorer transit systems, which are innovative bus systems targeted at tourists.

Although CMAQ funds are primarily used for projects in nonattainment areas, funds may also be used for projects in proximity to nonattainment and maintenance areas if benefits will be realized primarily within the nonattainment or maintenance area.[10] This is particularly relevant to rural areas that may not be directly eligible but may be the source of commuters to a nonattainment area. Transit agencies in Pennsylvania reported such use of CMAQ funds to develop park and ride facilities in an attainment area that served commuters to a nonattainment area and thus reduced VMT for that nonattainment area.

States without nonattainment areas, such as Iowa, still receive a minimum level of CMAQ funds that is considered flexible. This means that the funds are available for projects that are eligible for either CMAQ or STP and that do not meet CMAQ priority provisions. However, FTA and FWHA encourage targeting such funds to projects that reduce particulate matter.[11] The Iowa Transportation Commission recently directed Iowa DOT to start a new program to allocate CMAQ funding based on an application

---

5   For additional information, visit http://www dot gov/recovery/ost/faqs htm

6   For additional information, visit http://www fta dot gov/assistance/research_11424 html

7   For additional information, visit http://www fhwa dot gov/safetealu/factsheets/stp htm

8   For additional information, visit http://www fhwa dot gov/research/partnership/spr/

9   For additional information, visit http://www fhwa dot gov/environment/air_quality/cmaq/

10   The Congestion Mitigation and Air Quality (CMAQ) Improvement Program under the Safe, Accountable, Flexible, Efficient Transportation Equity Act: A Legacy for Users Final Program Guidance October 2008 http://www fhwa dot gov/environment/air_quality/cmaq/policy_and_guidance/cmaq08gd pdf

11   Ibid

process for projects that will maintain the State's attainment status by, for example, reducing emissions and VMT.

Other Federal Funding

There are a number of other Federal programs that provide significant funding for rural transit, especially when it provides human services transportation. Although this study is not intended to provide a comprehensive list of such funding sources, it does highlight use of related funds by participants in case study States. For example, Washington reports working with the Veteran's Administration to cover veterans' transit fares and as mentioned previously, Pennsylvania RPOs have successfully worked to implement the LUTED Initiative through their CEDS, funded by the Economic Development Administration.

Several States note that in addition to funding from FTA Sections 5310, 5316, and 5317, their coordinated plans incorporate Federal human services funding, including Medicaid, Administration on Aging, and Temporary Assistance for Needy Families programs, among other sources. Such funding comes either directly from Federal agencies or indirectly through State agencies (see next section), statewide human service transportation brokerages (Iowa and South Carolina), or health providers. One RPO in South Carolina reported using U.S. Department of Labor Workforce Investment Act (WIA)[12] funding as the local match for their Section 5316 JARC program. Another RPO in South Carolina is successfully combining U.S. DOT and USDHHS grants to fund an Aging, Disability, and Transportation Resource Center.

---

12 For additional information, visit http://www.doleta.gov/usworkforce/WIA/

State Funding

The case study States reported a range of funding for transit. Four of the case studies identified a designated source of transit funding, using a percentage of a user tax to fund transit: motor vehicles sales (Iowa and Minnesota), fuel (South Carolina), and highway tolls (Pennsylvania). Other States are constitutionally restricted to only using user fees for roads and bridges, so must draw upon other sources. Arizona used a percent of lottery proceeds for transit until 2010, when the State government redirected the funds to the General Fund. Some draw transit funding directly from the General Fund (Maine and Georgia) or appropriate funds into a State transit fund (Iowa, Minnesota). State funding is mostly focused on capital and planning (Washington and Georgia), with only some States providing funding for operations (Pennsylvania and, formerly, Arizona), placing the burden on Federal and local support.

Some State funding is provided by agencies outside of DOT. Two States (Maine and Georgia) reported that their departments that oversee health and human services contract directly with transportation providers to provide human services transportation. In Maine, some of the regional transportation providers only receive funding from the Maine Department of Health and Human Services. Since 1988, the Georgia DHS has managed the Section 5310 Program. Other departments, such as the Georgia Department of Labor, contract with DHS to provide transportation services for their clients. Initially, DHS focused on purchasing vehicles to provide service, but has since changed to purchasing services from existing providers, including Sections 5311 and 5307 (Urbanized Area Formula) systems.

Local Funding

Local funding for transit as reported by case study participants consists primarily of fares, contract fees for human service transportation, and tax or allocations from local governments. For example, transit agencies in Iowa reported having contracts to provide service to schools, Head Start programs, daycare facilities, nursing homes, and senior/assisted living centers. Four of the case study States provided examples of locally-imposed sales and use tax to support transit projects; two of the case study States do not provide State funding for operations.

In Washington, local communities or counties may vote to tax themselves to cover the costs of transit. Those areas that approve such a tax are termed public transportation benefits authorities (PTBAs). PBTAs were recently allowed to designate up to 9/10 of 1 percent, an increase from 6/10, of the sales tax to be directed toward public transportation. Only a few places have successfully adopted the increase. Georgia recently authorized a similar system, under the Transportation Investment Act of 2010, in which regional districts throughout the State may vote to implement a 1 percent sales tax for transportation projects, including transit projects.

In Maine, the State legislature recently passed legislation[13] for transit-oriented tax increment financing (TIF) districts, which amended State TIF regulations to allow local governments to use increased tax revenue from designated corridors or areas to create or improve transit, bicycle, and pedestrian facilities, including transit operator salaries, fuel, and maintenance, as well as transit-oriented development.

In South Carolina, TriCounty Link, a rural bus system for the counties of Berkeley, Charleston,

and Dorchester, was founded in 1996 with $30,000 in annual funding commitments from each county for three years. Following the three years, service was expected to become self-sufficient, which it did through providing Medicaid and contract services. The service now receives a half cent sales tax revenue commitment from Charleston County as a result of a referendum. The 20-year commitment has allowed TriCounty Link to provide additional services.

Local Match

The local match (20 percent) required for Federal funding is a concern for all case study States. Some States offer financial or advocacy support. Georgia provides half of the required match and ADOT staff attends local government meetings to promote transit, but for the most part, the task falls to the transit agency and its local government. As mentioned above, some transit agencies have had success using non-U.S. DOT Federal funding as a match.

MaineDOT provides one example of a State program that encourages local funding for transit, using a transit bonus payment[14] under the Urban-Rural Initiative Program (URIP),[15] which provides funds for capital improvements to local roads and rural State Aid minor collector roads. If a municipality with a fixed-route transit service that meets certain requirements increases its local funding for transit after the base year of FY2001, MaineDOT provides a "bonus" in URIP road funding equivalent to what is budgeted over and above the FY2001 transit budget. Thus, the "bonus" given toward road funding is based on the community's contribution to transit. The intent is for the municipality to be able to increase its support of transit, while not necessarily decreasing the funding it has available for road and bridge projects.

---

13 For information on An Act to Promote Economic Development and Reduce Reliance on Automobiles through Transit-Oriented Tax Increment Financing Districts, visit http://www.mainelegislature.org/ros/LOM/LOM124th/124R1/PUBLIC314.asp

14 http://www.maine.gov/sos/cec/rules/17/chaps17.htm

15 For additional information, visit http://www.maine.gov/mdot/community-programs/uri-program.php

Partnerships

Transit service is often supported by a number of agencies and entities. Most transit agencies receive Federal and State transportation funding, as well as local and human services funding. Some transit agencies, however, are also supported by and collaborate with other entities, such as universities, businesses, and Federal land management agencies such as the NPS. Maine and South Carolina both provide examples of these types of partnerships.

In Maine, Acadia National Park's Island Explorer transit service is the result of a partnership between the park, a nonprofit that supports the park, the local transit operator, and local towns and businesses. Funding has been provided by MaineDOT, FTA, FHWA, the Department of the Interior, towns, and local businesses, including L.L. Bean, a major Maine-based clothing and outdoor recreation equipment retail company. The NPS supplied the initial buses while MaineDOT, using CMAQ funds, provided the initial operating funds.

In South Carolina, transit providers reported on successful economic development initiatives that involved working with developers, universities, and businesses. For example, one transit agency reported that it struck a deal with a developer of condominiums to serve the site with transit in return for integrating transit infrastructure into the development, such as turnarounds and bus shelters. Another transit agency worked with a local employer to establish a commuter service with park and ride shuttles. Two other agencies worked with local universities to establish and then expand local public transit service.

2.6 Service

As reflected in the above continuum, baseline provision of service for rural transit covers a service area within a single jurisdiction, usually a county, and is targeted to human service and transit-dependent clients who are served by separate vehicles or providers. Advanced or evolving provision of rural transit consists of combined human service and public transportation that is provided to choice riders as well as transit-dependent riders and covers a broader geographic service area that is multi-county, intercity, and rural to urban.

The case study States all demonstrate advanced and evolving rural transit service. Common themes include multi-county regionalization, intercity bus and rail efforts, commuting service provision, coordination of human service and public transportation, and outreach to expand the coverage of rural transit. However, challenges remain around jurisdictional boundaries, especially interstate; funding restrictions on riders and destinations; and changing the public's perception of transit. The next section describes these topics and how some transit agencies have found successful ways to address them.

Many of the case study States provide demand response public transportation services in nearly all counties and all are working to expand coverage. Georgia and South Carolina provide two examples of outreach specific to rural areas to encourage transit service. GDOT sends an annual letter to all county governments that do not have Section 5311 programs to invite them to contact the Public Transportation Coordinator (PTC) in their region to discuss starting a Section 5311 program. GDOT also requires each PTC to conduct a follow-up phone call to those governments that do not respond. Similarly, SCDOT has offered the seven counties (as of 2009) that do not offer any general public transit an opportunity to receive funding for three-year pilot projects. Once the pilot is over, the services will be reviewed to determine how they performed, and whether or not they will become permanent and be included in the normal funding process.

Case study States vary in the extent of their implementation of regional, multi-county transit systems, but all demonstrate some exploration of regionalization. Iowa and Maine both have designated regional transit systems. Georgia has three pilot regional systems incorporated into the RPO structure, and South Carolina has eight regional transit authorities. Most of these efforts have been motivated by a desire to coordinate and consolidate human services and public transportation services to improve efficiency. In Maine for example, the nine designated regional transportation providers are non-profits that primarily provide demand-response and human service transportation services within their respective regions and manage all Section 5310 funds for their region. Pennsylvania recently completed a study to assess human service transportation coordination that recommended regional consolidation of management and service delivery. There are concerns about whether this is appropriate for all areas and if there could be other areas of improvement. Human service transportation can also be provided regionally or statewide through brokerages that exist alongside regional systems, such as in Iowa and South Carolina.

Intercity bus services – public or private – are a critical link to rural transit service that provide residents with transportation options and access to key destinations, including work, health care, and education statewide and across State borders. On the public side, Arizona and South Carolina provide examples of systems focused on job access. The Northern Arizona Intergovernmental Public Transportation Authority is a regional transportation system similar to those described above. Its focus is on commuting; it connects a small urban area (Flagstaff) with two rural communities (Sedona and Cottonwood). The western part of the State has been working on a similar system for the rural communities of Bullhead City, Kingman, and Lake Havasu, but funding is a challenge. Similarly, in South Carolina, the SmartRide Commuter-Focused Transit Program (http://www.dot.state.sc.us/getting/smartride/smartride.shtml) is a partnership between SCDOT, the Newberry County Council on Aging, and the Santee Wateree Regional Transit Authority

that provides commuter service to Columbia from Camden/Lugoff and Newberry, all small towns with populations under 50,000.

Several case study States, including Maine, Washington, and Georgia, report collaborative relationships with the intercity bus companies that serve their States. GDOT contracts with two intercity bus providers and leases buses developed under a State contract to them, with certain stipulations, such as limitations on out-of-state hours and the requirement of quarterly maintenance and ridership reports. Once a bus reaches the end of its useful life, the Georgia Department of Administrative Services holds an auction and the two providers often buy the buses to use for spare parts.

In terms of passenger rail, the case study States report progress in developing services that connect rural to urban areas across regions, the State, and multiple States. In Minnesota, the Northstar Commuter Rail Line (http://www.northstartrain.org/) is an example of a major passenger rail project linking rural, small urban, and large metropolitan areas. Opened in November 2009, the 40-mile Northstar Line connects downtown Minneapolis with suburbs within the metropolitan region and small non-urbanized towns northwest of the city. Arizona has a number of passenger rail initiatives underway, ranging from intra-region to intrastate and interstate. Regional entities throughout the State are conducting feasibility studies and creating implementation strategies to establish commuter rail in existing and new rail corridors in both rural and urban areas. ADOT received a Federal Railroad Administration (FRA) grant to conduct an environmental overview of eight conceptual rail corridors connecting Metropolitan Phoenix with Metropolitan Tucson as well as the dozen rural communities located within the corridors. Finally, in partnership with California and Nevada, Arizona is participating in a FRA-funded high-speed rail study.

Linky, a Low Country tree frog and popular TriCounty Link mascot – South Carolina
Photograph provided by SR Concepts

Chapter 3: Observations and Challenges

This section describes several common themes that emerged from the case studies, with examples. This is not a comprehensive analysis of the detailed research in the case studies, but serves to highlight the key themes that emerged as most prevalent and relevant to the study, and were not covered in the categories above. The themes featured are:

- Success in the context of limited and constrained resources

- Changing perceptions of rural transit

- Performance measures

- Tribal transit

3.1 Success in the Context of Limited and Constrained Resources

Case study participants reported that they are consistently being challenged by the limited availability and flexibility of funding and staff, population growth, and long distances. These challenges have direct impacts on the ability of a transit agency to provide service that meets community needs and goals. However, some rural transit agencies are finding successful ways to combat these challenges.

Availability of Funding

Availability of funding is limited for rural transit at the Federal, State, and local levels but is particularly difficult when the State source is not dedicated and protected, such as what occurred in Arizona in 2010 when lottery proceeds were redirected from transit to the General Fund. The local match, as mentioned above, is also a main challenge especially for rural

communities. Funding can also be made difficult by the need for rural transit to compete not only with other rural transit but also with highway and bridge projects and urban transit.

Funding Flexibility

Funding flexibility can be an issue because of rules that either prohibit or make it administratively onerous to provide service across jurisdictions, combine multiple funding programs, and combine human services and public transportation trips and riders. Consistent boundaries between DOT, RPO, and other designated State districts would help in reducing staff time needed to pursue funding. Washington's consolidated grant process and application allows applicants to submit one application for Federal and State programs.

New Systems and Small MPOs

The problem of funding is viewed as particularly acute for new systems and new small MPOs. New small MPOs occur in areas of rapid population growth, mostly in western States and in non-urbanized areas near urban centers. If a community has not established a transit system prior to receiving MPO designation, it loses its chance to access operations funding through the Section 5311 program. In order to prevent this, ADOT has been proactive in encouraging formation of new transit systems in non-urbanized areas that are approaching a population of 50,000, so as to access operating funds and prepare for the additional requirements and funding opportunities that will be made available to the community once its population surpasses 50,000.

Long Distances

Long distances between destinations and from major population centers contribute to increased operating costs, restrict access to training and skilled staff, and limit the ability to participate in State and regional meetings. Although ADOT staff attempt to conduct field visits and attend local meetings in person, they rely on the RPOs to help with outreach and have increased their use of webinars and voice and email communications. Additionally, ADOT has begun developing a network of certified trainers so that professional improvement courses and other transit training can be conducted locally, reducing travel by transit professionals to Phoenix or Tucson. PennDOT and the Pennsylvania Public Transit Association are both credited by rural transit agencies with successfully communicating despite geographic distances.

3.2 Changing Perceptions of Rural Transit

Case study participants report that perceptions of transit in rural areas are becoming more positive as rural transit agencies, with the support of SDOTs, RPOs, and others, are having success communicating to the public – as well as government officials – the important role that rural transit can play in economic development, the environment, and quality of life. However, participants also noted it is equally important to communicate the costs associated with such benefits.

Outreach Tools

As mentioned previously, the success in changing perception stems in part from efforts on marketing, education, and innovative services. Marketing requires a balance between communicating the need for financial support and providing professional, desirable services. Education related to the benefits of rural transit investments has primarily focused on the role of transit in enabling communities to

grow and the benefits of reduced air pollution and GHG emissions. Innovative services focused on employment or other destinations and provision of a convenient and enjoyable experience attract choice riders while also supporting transit-dependent riders.

Combined Strategies

TriCounty Link in South Carolina has had success using all three strategies to promote its service. First, the agency hired a community outreach person who travels throughout the region to educate people on the difference transit can make. Second, the agency changed its name from the Berkeley, Charleston, Dorchester Rural Transportation Management Authority (BCD-RTMA) to TriCounty Link and adopted a new logo and mascot, Linky. Third, TriCounty Link developed a high-frequency lunch-time circulator service in an employment center and set up a reciprocal commuter agreement with Charleston Area Rapid Transit Authority (CARTA), which means TriCounty Link passengers are now able to transfer at no-cost between TriCounty Link services and CARTA, and vice versa.

SDOT Support

SDOTs can positively impact the perception of rural transit in a variety of ways, including advocating at local meetings, conducting studies that demonstrate the benefits of transit in all areas, and providing incentives in terms of funding or technical support. States have used websites to make information about transit, including rural transit, more accessible to the public. Two of the case study States provide successful examples of websites that provide the public with information on the availability and benefits of transit. PennDOT operates and maintains an interactive map website (http://www. dot.state.pa.us/BPTMAP/index.htm) that displays what services are provided by each county and provides county listings of transit operators and services. This website makes it easy for residents to identify where transit is available, even in isolated areas. MaineDOT's Explore Maine website (http://www.exploremaine.org) provides comprehensive information about the wide variety of reliable travel options (air, bike, bus, car, ferry, and train) and connectivity between modes within Maine, with an emphasis on how to access remote places otherwise inaccessible by car.

3.3 Performance Measures

Four of the case study States (SC, GA, IA, and WA) reported using some type of performance measures for transit in funding allocations. South Carolina, Iowa, and Washington all use performance measures in allocating FTA Sections 5310 and 5311 funds. Iowa also uses performance measures to allocate State transit funding. The performance-based formulas include measures of passenger trips, farebox recovery, miles, and cost. Georgia uses a small subset of measures as requirements for eligibility for Section 5311 and additional capital requests.

South Carolina and Washington both produce annual public performance reports for use by transit providers, the legislature, and local and regional governments. The reports allow both SDOTs

to track performance, provide transparency and accountability, inform the State legislature, guide State priorities and initiatives, and identify needs and challenges. For example, SCDOT's Transit Trends report states that because of the rural nature of the State, there is a significant need to direct resources to the particular challenges of rural transit. Minnesota also has an annual performance report that covers all transportation. It includes bus service hours as a measure for rural transit. The Greater Minnesota Transit Plan similarly contains performance targets for service hours to meet 80 percent of the State's estimated demand for public transit. Minnesota has found that it is necessary to think differently about performance measures for rural as opposed to urban transit because of the characteristics of rural transit, such as distance and purpose, as described previously.

In Iowa, transit agencies submit quarterly reports on progress in terms of the selected performance measures, while Georgia transit agencies submit a monthly report used internally by GDOT and transit agencies to track progress toward goals and service performance, and identify any issues.

Figure 6. Intermodal Transportation Center in Sumter, SC

Source: Santee Wateree Regional Transit Authority

3.4 Tribal Transit

Throughout the U.S., a growing number of Tribal governments provide transit in rural areas. Of the case study States, four (AZ, ME, SC, and WA) shared experiences of working with Tribal governments on rural transit. Although this study is not focused on Tribal transit, it is important to recognize that it plays an integral and significant role in rural transit. Participants recognized this fact and the challenges and opportunities Tribal transit provides for statewide planning for rural transit.

Of the case study States, Arizona has the most significant Tribal presence. There are 22 Federally-recognized Tribes, which control nearly a third of the State's land and which are predominantly located in rural areas. The former ADOT Public Transportation Division Director firmly stated that Tribes are very important for Arizona. The current ADOT Multimodal Planning Division Director clearly stated that one "cannot talk about rural transit in Arizona without talking about Tribal transit." Three Tribes have systems funded by Section 5311 and at least five have been recipients of the Tribal Transit Program. Most Tribal transit services, however, are provided by the Elder Programs of each Tribe, through the Section 5310 program.

Several SDOTs and RPOs reported working with local Tribes on transportation, although transit was more limited in part due to the nature of the Tribal Transit Program, which does not require coordination of the application process with the SDOT or by its recipients with other transit entities. However, there have been a number of successes. The Yakima Nation in Washington contracts with a private non-profit to run its system, which is funded by the Tribal Transit Program and connects with the rest of the non-profit's system within the City of Yakima, as well as the transit system for the adjacent Tri-Cities (Kennewick, Pasco, and Richland). Within Arizona, the extensive presence of such Tribal transit has resulted in several statewide interagency partnerships and engagement efforts by ADOT, including the Arizona Tribal Strategic Partnering Team[16] and support of the 2009 National Tribal Transit Conference.[17] Despite these successes, there are still opportunities to improve access to funding and technical assistance, staffing, coordination across jurisdictions, and development of relationships.

16   For additional information, visit http://www.aztribaltransportation org/ATSPT/index asp

17   For additional information, visit http://www.navajotransit com/component/content/article/1-latest-news/47-tribal-transit-conference-2009 html

Georgia Regional Transportation Authority Xpress
Source: Volpe Center

STREET ELEVATION

A NEW INTERMODAL FACILITY
FOR CLEMSON AREA TRANSIT
CLEMSON, S.C.

Detail of a rendering of the Clemson Area Transit Intermodal Facility – South Carolina
Provided by Clemson Area Transit

Chapter 4: The Role of Transit in Rural Livability

This section presents observations and insights from the study into how statewide transportation planning can strengthen the role transit plays in creating livable rural communities. Statewide planning guides transportation resource allocation decisions that play a major role in creating livable communities in rural areas — from meeting basic mobility and accessibility needs to supporting economic development and provision of health and human services. This section considers how those entities that are directly or indirectly involved in the provision of rural transit participate in transportation planning that supports livability through rural transit, and presents relevant best practice examples from the Transit at the Table III case studies.

4.1 Defining Livability for Rural Transit

This description of transit's contribution to livability in rural communities builds from several key resources, listed at the end of the document, including the Livability Principles of the DOT-HUD-EPA Partnership for Sustainable Communities:

- Enhance economic competitiveness

- Support existing communities

- Provide more transportation choices

- Value communities and neighborhoods

- Promote equitable, affordable housing

- Coordinate policies and leverage investment

This section identifies how SDOTs, RPOs, transit agencies, and local communities use planning to support transit's advancement of the Livability Principles. Although these entities may not directly identify "livability" as their priority, they consistently articulate goals related to key elements of livability — preserving rural community identity, and retaining and attracting residents, employers, and visitors, by providing transit options to important destinations.

As demonstrated in the Transit at the Table III case studies, rural transit can meet livability goals by providing equitable access to work, education, health services, and other destinations, particularly for residents with limited mobility options because of income, age, health, geographic isolation, or other factors. By broadening access, rural transit plays a major role in the health, quality of life, and economic viability of rural communities.

This research identifies three key themes for how planning can support transit's contribution to rural livability:

Accessibility

- Although transit is one, often relatively small component of rural transportation networks, it provides service, including through intermodal connections, that addresses equity, quality of life, and access to lifeline services.

- Transit is a critical link to key destinations in rural livable communities: jobs, community and health services, affordable housing, education, and natural, cultural, and recreational opportunities.

- Access is a significant challenge for rural communities because of long distances between destinations, which can require mobility across large regions or between dispersed urban and rural areas.

Economic Development and Community Preservation

- Rural communities depend on economic development to preserve their character and vitality. Transit contributes by improving access to jobs and services and sustaining or attracting growth and services.

- Transit further assists rural communities to enhance economic viability by retaining and attracting new residents and employers through expanding transportation choices and reducing congestion and pollution.

Environmental Sustainability

- Environmental sustainability is closely related to the quality of life in rural communities — transit contributes to improved air quality, reduced GHG emissions, and increased energy efficiency.

This section draws upon research for Transit at the Table III to explore how these themes can be advanced by rural transit, supported by statewide transportation planning and its varied participants.

4.2 Livability and Statewide Planning for Rural Transit

Chapter 2 identifies five ways in which statewide transportation planning considers and supports rural transit. These aspects of planning strengthen transit's ability to contribute to livability in rural communities. For example, State livability goals incorporated within the statewide planning process can support local decisions to direct flexible Federal transportation funds to rural transit investments that also meet local goals. These statewide goals, whether for balanced land use, environmental quality, or economic development, can be focused or expanded to also meet local needs. Table 3 provides a continuum of how livability can be achieved by rural transit in each of the five transportation planning categories, ranging from "early or basic" to "advanced or evolving" approaches identified by the study team.

4.3 Roles of Government

The contribution of transit to rural livability goals varies among the communities studied and involves multiple partners and investments of funds from multiple sources, reflecting the diversity of these communities. This study found that different entities play different roles in planning for rural transit, including in pursuit of livability goals.

Federal

A number of Federal agencies, including the Departments of Transportation, Agriculture, Interior, Health and Human Services, and Commerce (specifically the Economic Development Agency), are integral to supporting economic development and access to medical services and employment in rural areas. For U.S. DOT, this study focused on FTA rather than other DOT modal agencies.

State

DOTs and other State agencies support rural livability through statewide transportation planning by setting statewide livability goals; incorporating livability criteria into expenditure of funds from State and Federal programs; directly designating funds or creating incentives or requirements to expand transit and intercity bus programs; providing technical assistance and training; and conducting studies.

Regional

Many RPOs or other similar regional agencies provide significant links between land use and transportation, including transit; RPOs are often responsible for community and economic development and other programs and can support SDOTs by providing technical assistance, training, and allocation of funding to local communities.

Local

Local governments and transit agencies report success in partnering with businesses and universities, conducting marketing campaigns to change the perception of transit, and leveraging non-transportation funding opportunities to improve how rural transit supports economic development, quality of life, and access.

4.4 Case Study Examples

This study identified a broad range of ways in which State, regional, local agencies, and transit providers participate in statewide transportation planning to ensure that transit supports livability in rural areas. These activities meet the Livability Principles, occur within the planning framework described above, and provide a valuable resource for peer State, regional, and local agencies. Examples include:

- Georgia's DHS and SDOT coordinate to direct Federal funding to rural transit and designate staff to participate in regional coordinated human transportation service committees, which develop the plans required for Federal funding. These committees are creating long-lasting and effective partnerships between public health and transportation officials that will help ensure access to health care services by all, including those with low incomes.

- PennDOT's LUTED Initiative has led RPOs to incorporate regional LUTED plans into their LRTP and CEDS, which are Federally-funded by the Economic Development Administration. As a result, RPOs are able to use different funding sources and take a more comprehensive approach to planning and programming projects that address access and economic development.

- ADOT reports a new emphasis in statewide plans on livability, including Complete Streets concepts and shifting commutes from rural areas to urban areas from highway to public transportation — both intercity bus and rail — to address job access and air quality.

This summary highlights how the transportation planning process in three States supports livability through rural transit. The full case studies for these and five other States can be found online at the FTA/FHWA Transportation Capacity Building website (http://www.planning.dot.gov/).

Table 3. Continuum of How Statewide Transportation Planning Supports Rural Transit and Livability

Category	Baseline (Basic Approach)	Advanced/Evolving Approach
Goals	Mobility and accessibility for transit-dependent populations	Livability and sustainability: community-wide economic development, equity, environment, multimodal and intermodal connections
Planning Products and Processes	Plans and processes focus on mobility, safety, and air quality	Plans that incorporate livability goals and funding processes that include livability criteria
Institutional Relationships	Limited interactions for funding and compliance between DOT and transit agency	Informal and formal collaboration and two-way communication across multiple entities and jurisdictions
Funding	FTA programs	Leveraging of other sources, including non-DOT public and private
Service	On-demand, intra-jurisdictional service to medical and other human services	Regularly scheduled, regional and intercity service to a variety of destinations

Maine

MaineDOT's statewide LRTP, Connecting Maine (2008),[18] identifies economic development, as well as sustainability and connections to land use, as goals for transportation. The plan's framework consists of 38 Corridors of Regional Economic Significance for Transportation focused on multi-modal intercity connections, but many of the cities are classified as rural or the corridors pass through rural areas. In addition, MaineDOT has supported the creation of innovative Island Explorer bus shuttle systems, which are intended to advance local economies by attracting and serving tourists while also meeting local community needs, including access to jobs and improved air quality. For example, the Island Explorer, which serves Acadia National Park, meets both MaineDOT's economic development goal and the NPS's visitor

experience and environmental quality goals by providing transportation for tourists, tourism industry workers, and fisherman.[19]

MaineDOT has also promoted rural transit and transportation choices through its website, Explore Maine (http://www.exploremaine.org/), which provides comprehensive information about the wide variety of reliable travel options (air, bike, bus, car, ferry, and train) and connectivity between modes within Maine, with an emphasis on how to access remote places otherwise inaccessible by car. The promotion of alternative transportation is consistent with the Maine Climate Action Plan (http://www.maine.gov/dep/air/greenhouse/), which also promotes effective land use decisions and lists transit ridership as a potential performance measure.

18 For additional information, visit http://www.maine gov/mdot/connectingmaine/index htm

19 See FTA's rural livability showcase study, http://fta dot gov/documents/maine pdf

Figure 7. Left: Island Explorer, Downeast Transportation/Acadia National Park. Right: WSDOT Sustainable Transportation

Source: Volpe Center

Source: WSDOT

Washington

Washington State takes a proactive approach to integrating transportation, including rural transit, with sustainability, climate change, livability goals, policies, and programs. Under the 2009 Executive Order 09-05 Washington's Leadership on Climate Change,[20] the State Departments of Ecology, Transportation, and Commerce collaborate in a manner similar to the DOT-HUD-EPA Partnership for Sustainable Communities, but with a specific charge to identify strategies to reduce VMT and GHG emissions from the transportation sector while considering air quality and impacts on the economy.

One way in which WSDOT supports this initiative is by promoting carpooling, vanpooling, and public transportation services, including intercity bus. The State vanpooling program is not limited to urban areas: several rural regions also take advantage of the program. For example, Job Lift (http://www2.olycap.org/Employment_Assistance.php) is a partnership vanpool program with Olympic Community Action Program and Clallam Transit that provides transportation to low-income individuals living in Olympic Peninsula's rural western areas. The program, supported by the State and FTA's JARC grant program, consists of three vanpools providing service that includes up to 45 trips a day to low-income individuals, giving them access to job sites, training, and interviews, as well as daycare.[21] Intercity bus provides a critical link with rural transit service to provide residents with transportation options and access to key

destinations statewide, including work, health care, and education sites. Good communication and coordination by the providers, combined with small but targeted investment by WSDOT, has led to a successful network that helps support rural communities.

Figure 8. Job Lift Van Pool Program — Washington

Source: Olympic Community Action Program

South Carolina

South Carolina has examples at the State, regional, and local levels that reflect the incorporation of livability into project prioritization, funding, and the provision of everyday transit services. In April 2010, FHWA South Carolina Division, in partnership with SCDOT, FTA, and a number of other Federal agencies, hosted a workshop entitled "Beginning the Conversation about Livability." The event resulted in an open and lively discussion about livability, what it means, and how it can become an integral part of future transportation planning efforts in South Carolina.

At the State level, consideration of transit accommodation, or transit as an alternative to the project, is required criterion for the prioritization

---

20 For additional information, visit http://www.governor.wa.gov/execorders/eo_09-05.pdf

21 For information on rural transit and livability in Mason County, to the south, see FTA's rural livability showcase study, http://fta.dot.gov/documents/Rural_MasonCounty.pdf

Figure 9. Aging, Disability, and Transportation Resource Center Ribbon Cutting and Vehicle.

Sources: Fast Lane (U.S. Secretary of Transportation Blog and Susan Richards, SR Concepts)

and ranking of projects to be funded in the STIP. In addition, communities are able to add their own criteria to the project selection process, including livability criteria such as improving access to public and civic destinations, resulting in connectivity and open space; creating walkable neighborhoods; or investing in established communities.

Regional agencies are able to leverage SCDOT and Federal funding to provide improved access to health care and jobs through provision of rural transit. The Lower Savannah Council of Governments has combined U.S. DOT and U.S. Department of Health and Human Services grants to fund an Aging, Disability, and Transportation Resource Center and equip transit vehicles throughout the region with intelligent transportation systems technology. Federal funding sources for the project include a 2005 transformation grant[22] from the Centers for Medicare and Medicaid, facilitated by the Lieutenant Governor's Office of Aging; U.S. DOT Mobility Services for All

Americans Initiative (http://www.its.dot.gov/msaa/) planning and implementation grants; and ARRA funding for the building. Similarly, SCDOT provided FTA Section 5304 (Statewide Planning) funding to support a successful FTA Bus Livability grant application by Lowcountry Council of Governments, Lowcountry Regional Transportation Authority, Beauford County, and the University of South Carolina at Beaufort. The grant will help fund local circulator service that is also being supported by nearby military facilities and the local tourism industry.

Local transit agencies in particular have been able to both promote and leverage livability goals to partner with universities and employers to provide expanded service. TriCounty Link, which provides service to three counties in southeast South Carolina, has found success in changing people's perception of transit as a desirable choice by providing convenient and innovative services, such as no-cost transfers with the CARTA, free wireless on its commuter buses, and the innovative

---

22 For additional information about Transformation Grants, visit https://www.cms.gov/MedicaidTransGrants/

Figure 10. TriCounty Link's Link to Lunch Service

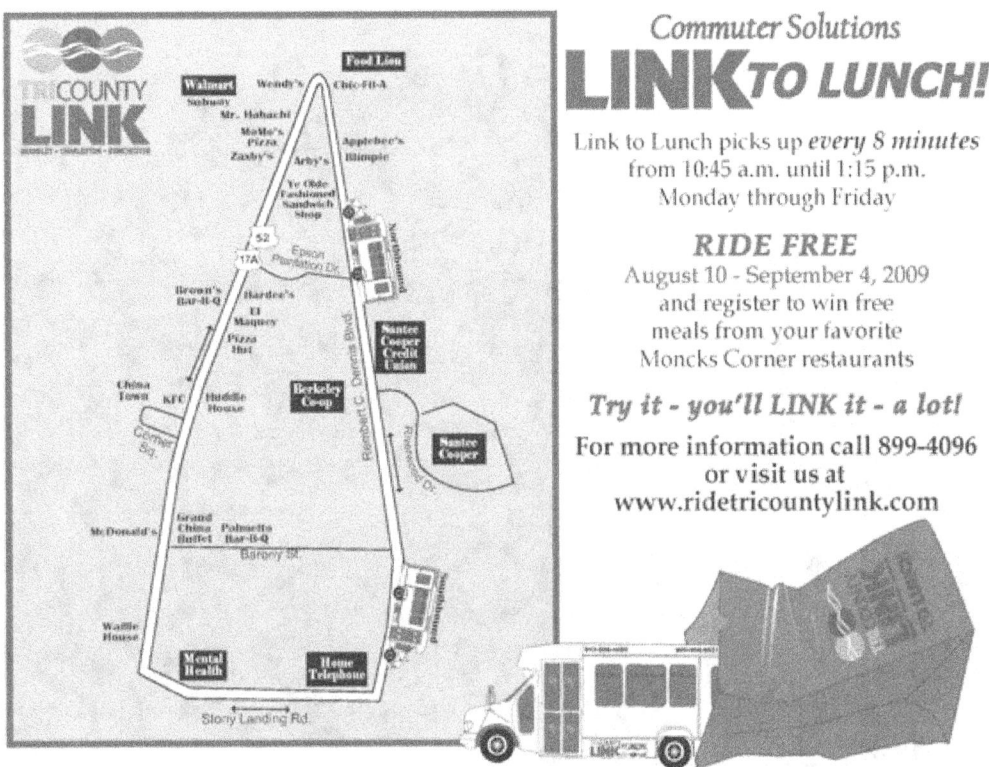

Source: TriCounty Link (http://www.ridetricountylink.com/downloads/TCL-LinkToLunchFlyer-080409.pdf)

Link to Lunch[23] service, providing weekday trips to lunch sites for workers and other residents.

4.5 Conclusion

By considering the role of transit in rural communities, statewide transportation planning can make important contributions to the livability of these communities. This chapter showcases many of the ways that statewide planning, with active participation by State, regional, and local partners, can support transit and more livable, rural communities. This document summarizes insights related to planning, transit, and rural livability from research conducted for Transit at the Table III. FTA hopes that the examples highlighted will assist SDOTs, RPOs, local governments, and transit agencies to plan for transit that will improve livability in rural communities nationwide.

---

23 For additional information, visit http://www.ridetricountylink.com/commuterRoutes/LinktoLunch.html

Island Explorer, Acadia National Park – Maine
Photograph provided by the Volpe Center

APPENDIX A:
Self-Assessment Checklist
for Transit Operators

Key findings from the study, *Transit at the Table III: A Guide to Effective Participation in Statewide Decisionmaking for Transit Agencies in Non-Urbanized Areas* were used in preparing the following questions for transit operators in non-urbanized areas to use in assessing their role and participation in statewide planning. The indicators are generic and not exhaustive; therefore, these questions should be regarded as only the starting point for subsequent discussions targeted to specific opportunities within the local context.

While answering these questions may illuminate issues and opportunities for transit operators in non-urbanized areas, perhaps the greatest value of this work is in subsequent discussion among planning partners. The checklist may be applied effectively in facilitated group settings as a useful catalyst to discussion. "Yes" responses generally suggest more positive outcomes or experiences.

Transit Operator Participation in Metropolitan Transportation Planning

	YES	NO
1. Relationship with State DOT		
• Do you have an existing relationship with any State DOT (SDOT) official?	___	___
• Does your SDOT or State transit association organize a statewide public transportation conference?	___	___
• **If yes,** do you attend?	___	___
• Do you participate in any of the training provided by the SDOT or State transit association?	___	___

	YES	NO
2. Relationship with Regional Planning Organization (RPO) or Equivalent (e.g., Regional Planning Commission (RPC), Council of Governments (COG), and/or Metropolitan Planning Organization (MPO))		
• Do you know the name and location of your RPO?	___	___
• Do you have an existing relationship with any RPO staff or board members?	___	___
• Is there is a Memorandum of Understanding (MOU) between your agency and the RPO?	___	___
• **If yes:** Is that MOU up-to-date and reflective of policy, responsibility, and/or funding changes?	___	___
• **If yes:** Does the MOU identify explicit roles for transit operators in the statewide planning process?	___	___
• Are you a voting member of the RPO Board (or have Board representation)?	___	___
• Are you represented on, and active in, RPO policy and/or technical committees?	___	___

3. Relationship with Others

	YES	NO
• Do you have an existing relationship with the State transit association?	_____	_____
• Do you have an existing relationship with any local businesses, schools, universities, Tribes, or Federal land management agencies (e.g., National Parks)?	_____	_____
• Do you have an existing relationship with any local or regional human services agencies?	_____	_____

4. Involvement in Planning and Special Studies

	YES	NO
• Does your region have a long-range transportation plan (LRTP)?	_____	_____
• **If yes:** Are you involved in its development?	_____	_____
• **If yes:** Is there a transit component of the plan?	_____	_____
• Does your region have a rural planning work program or equivalent?	_____	_____
• **If yes:** Are you involved in its development?	_____	_____
• Does your region have a coordinated human services plan?	_____	_____
• **If yes:** Are you involved in its development?	_____	_____
• **If yes:** Does your region have a committee that meets regularly?	_____	_____
• Are you involved in developing the State LRTP?	_____	_____
• Do you monitor progress and products of the statewide planning process?	_____	_____
• Does the State transportation plan . . .		
• Integrate public transportation elements with highway, pedestrian, bicycle, air, and other modes?	_____	_____
• Address rural public transit?	_____	_____
• Include transit-supportive development policies and strategies?	_____	_____
• Include transportation system management, maintenance, and operations?	_____	_____
• Include plans/policies that highlight the benefits of transit?	_____	_____
• Consider economic development, job access, air quality, social services, human services transportation, health and safety, and/or historic preservation?	_____	_____
• Consider rural access to intercity bus or passenger rail?	_____	_____
• Include performance measures that are relevant to rural transit?	_____	_____
• Are you involved in educating the public or promoting regional comprehensive plans and politics?	_____	_____
• Are you involved in corridor studies to ensure that all modes are considered?	_____	_____

5. Involvement in Funding and Implementation

	YES	NO

- Do you understand the role of regional and State transportation improvement programs (TIPs) in the statewide planning process? _____ _____

- Do you know about the following Federal funding programs that your agency may be able to access through the State?

    - Congestion Mitigation and Air Quality (CMAQ; FTA/FHWA) _____ _____

    - Transportation Enhancement (FHWA) _____ _____

    - Section 5316 Job Access and Reverse Commute (FTA) _____ _____

    - Section 5317 New Freedom (FTA) _____ _____

    - Transportation Investments Generating Economic Recovery II Grants (U.S. DOT/HUD) _____ _____

    - Community Challenge Planning Grants (U.S. DOT/HUD) _____ _____

    - Workforce Investment Act (Department of Labor) _____ _____

    - Sustainable Communities Regional Planning Grants (HUD) _____ _____

    - Climate Showcase Communities (EPA) _____ _____

- Are you involved in identifying, prioritizing, and scheduling projects for the regional or statewide TIP? _____ _____

- Do you feel that the TIP prioritization process is objective and fact-based? _____ _____

- Do you feel that you receive a fair share of the region's project funding? _____ _____

- Is the State's status reporting of TIP project funding timely, understandable, and reliable? _____ _____

- Are you involved in cooperatively forecasting revenues for the regional and/or State LRTP and TIP? _____ _____

- Are your fares, grants, contracts, or other revenues considered and incorporated in these estimates? _____ _____

- Are you able to assume future revenue enhancement plans and proposals? _____ _____

Bullhead Area Transit System – Arizona
Photograph provided by Bullhead

APPENDIX B:
References and Resources

Relevant Websites:

- RPO America (http://www.ruraltransportation.org/)

- Rural and Small Community Transportation Planning (http://www.planning.dot.gov/rural.asp)

- National Rural Transit Assistance Program (http://www.nationalrtap.org/)

- United We Ride (http://www.unitedweride.gov/)

- The DOT-HUD-EPA Partnership for Sustainable Communities, in particular the Six Livability Principles (http://www.epa.gov/smartgrowth/partnership/)

- The FTA Livable and Sustainable Communities initiative (http://fta.dot.gov/publications/publications_10935.html)

Relevant Publications: (ordered from most recent to least recent)

Analysis of Statewide Long-Range Transportation Plans: Synthesis Report and Database. John A. Volpe National Transportation Systems Center for the Federal Highway Administration. http://planning.dot.gov/stateplans.

Public Transit Regional Coordination Pilot Projects in North Dakota. Upper Great Plains Transportation Institute, North Dakota State University. December 2010. http://www.ugpti.org/pubs/pdf/DP237.pdf

Livability in Transportation Guidebook: Planning Approaches that Promote Livability. Federal Highway Administration and Federal Transit Administration. 2010. http://www.fhwa.dot.gov/livability/case_studies/guidebook/livabilitygb10.pdf

Livability Case Studies and Outreach. Federal Transit Administration. 2010. http://fta.dot.gov/publications/publications_10991.html

Case Studies on Transit and Livable Communities in Rural and Small Town America. Transportation for America. March 2010. http://t4america.org/wp-content/uploads/2010/09/Livability-Transit-Rural-Case-Studies-WEB.pdf

Statewide Transportation Planning: Opportunities Exist to Transition to Performance-Based Planning and Federal Oversight. U.S. Government Accountability Office. December 2010. http://www.gao.gov/special.pubs/gao-11-78sp/index.htm

Getting Back on Track: Aligning State Transportation Policy with Climate Change Goals. Smart Growth America & Natural Resources Defense Council. December 2010. http://www.nrdc.org/smartgrowth/files/GettingBackonTrack_report.pdf

Webinar: Transportation, Small Towns, and Rural Regions. Transportation for America. May 14, 2009. www.t4america.org/webinars. http://t4america.org/policybriefs/t4_policybrief_rural.pdf

Current Practice and Future Guidance on the Development of SAFETEA-LU-Required Coordinated Public Transit-Human Services Transportation Plans. NCHRP Project 20-65, Task 14. April 2009. http://onlinepubs.trb.org/onlinepubs/nchrp/nchrp_rrd_331.pdf

Metropolitan and Rural Transportation Planning: Case Studies and Checklists for Regional Collaboration. National Association of Development Organizations (NADO). January 2009. http://www.ruraltransportation.org/uploads/rpompo.pdf

Research Foundation and Association of Metropolitan Planning Organizations (AMPO) with support from the Federal Highway Administration. January 2009. http://66.132.139.69/uploads/rpompo.pdf

CTAA Magazine Edition: Transit for Rural America. Community Transportation Association of America. 2008. http://web1.ctaa.org/webmodules/webarticles/anmviewer.asp?a=155&z=5

Public Transportation on the Move in Rural America. U.S. Department of Agriculture. 2008. http://www.nal.usda.gov/ric/ricpubs/publictrans.htm

Rural Local Officials Consultation Assessment Guide: Evaluating Your Knowledge and Input into the Statewide Transportation on Planning Process. National Association of Development Organizations (NADO) Research Foundation. September 2008. http://www.ruraltransportation.org/uploads/assess08.pdf

Transportation Planning in Rural America: Emerging Models for Local Consultation, Regional Coordination and Rural Planning Organizations. National Association of Development Organizations Research Foundation. December 2005. http://66.132.139.69/uploads/scan2005.pdf

Current State Issues with Implementing FTA Section 5310 and 5311 Programs. NCHRP Project 20-65, Task 1. Research for the AASHTO Standing Committee on Public Transportation. December 2005. http://onlinepubs.trb.org/onlinepubs/nchrp/nchrp_rrd_320.pdf

TRCP Report 101: Toolkit for Rural Community Coordinated Transportation Services. 2004. http://www.transitaccessproject.org/InternalDocs/CoordinatedSystems/Toolkit%20for%20Rural%20 Community_TCRP_RPT_101.pdf

Local Government Officials: Key Stakeholders in Rural Transportation Planning. December 2004. NADO/NACO. http://66.132.139.69/uploads/leoprimer.pdf

Mobility for America's Small Urban and Rural Communities. American Public Transportation Association. 2003. http://lobby.la.psu.edu/_107th/125_SMART_Growth/Organizational_Statements/APTA/APTA_mobility_ for_urban_rural_commnties.htm

CTAA Magazine Edition: Rural America Needs Transit. Community Transportation Association of America. 2003. http://web1.ctaa.org/webmodules/webarticles/anmviewer.asp?a=203

APPENDIX C:
Non-SDOT Study
Participants

State	Type of Entity	Entity	Website
AZ	Other	Arizona Transit Association	http://www.azta.org/
AZ	Other	Inter Tribal Council of Arizona, Inc.	http://www.itcaonline.com/
AZ	RPO	Northern Arizona Council of Governments	http://www.nacog.org/
AZ	RPO	Northern Arizona Intergovernmental Public Transportation Authority	http://www.naipta.az.gov/
AZ	RPO	SouthEastern Arizona Governments Organization	http://www.seago.org/
AZ	Transit	Bullhead City / Bullhead Area Transit System	http://www.bullheadcity.com/
AZ	Transit	City of Cottonwood / Cottonwood Area	http://www.cat.az.gov/
AZ	Transit	City of Kingman / Kingman Area Transit	http://www.cityofkingman.gov/pages/depts/kart/
AZ	Transit	Pinal-Gila Council for Senior Citizens	http://www.pgcsc.org/
GA	RPO	Coastal Georgia Regional Commission	http://www.crc.ga.gov
GA	RPO	Three Rivers Regional Commission	http://www.threeriversrc.com/
GA	State	Department of Health and Human Services Region 4	http://www.hhs.gov/about/regions/index.html#r4
GA	Transit	Coweta County / Coweta Transit	http://www.coweta.ga.us/index.aspx?page=950
GA	Transit	Pierce County / Pierce County Transit	http://www.piercecountyga.org/Transit_files/Transit.htm
GA	Transit	Troup County	http://www.troupcountyga.org/
IA	RPO	Iowa Northland Regional Council of Governments	http://www.inrcog.org/
IA	RPO	Siouxland Interstate Metropolitan Planning Council	http://simpco.org/
IA	RPO	Southeast Iowa Regional Planning Commission	http://www.seirpc.com/
IA	Transit	River Bend Transit	http://www.riverbendtransit.org/
IA	Transit	Western Iowa Transit System	http://www.region12cog.org/western_iowa_public_transit/public_transit.asp
ME	RPO	Androscoggin Valley Council of Governments	http://www.avcog.org/
ME	Transit	Community Concepts	http://www.community-concepts.org/
ME	Transit	Downeast Transportation	http://www.downeasttrans.org/
ME	Transit	Penquis / The Lynx	http://www.penquis.org/
ME	Transit	York County Community Action	http://www.yccac.org/
MN	RPO	East Central Regional Development Commission (Region 7E)	http://www.region7erdc.org/
MN	RPO	Mid-Minnesota Development Commission (Region 6E)	http://www.mmrdc.org/
MN	RPO	Southwest Regional Development Commission	http://www.swrdc.org/
MN	Transit	Rainbow Rider Transit	http://www.rainbowriderbus.com/

State	Type of Entity	Entity	Website
MN	Transit	Tri-County Action Program (Tri-CAP)	http://www.tricap.org/transportation.html
PA	RPO	North Central Regional Planning and Development Commission	http://www.ncentral.com/
PA	RPO	Northern Tier Regional Planning and Development Commission	http://www.northerntier.org/
PA	RPO	SEDA-Council of Governments	http://www.seda-cog.org/Pages/Home.aspx
PA	Transit	Transportation Authority	http://www.catabus.com/
PA	Transit	Indiana County Transit Authority / IndiGO	http://www.indigobus.com/
PA	Transit	Monroe County Transit Authority / Pocono Pony	http://www.gomcta.com/
SC	RPO	Catawba Council of Governments	http://catawbacog.org/
SC	RPO	Central Midlands Council of Governments	http://www.centralmidlands.org/
SC	RPO	Lowcountry Council of Governments	http://lowcountrycog.sc.gov/
SC	RPO	Lower Savannah Council of Governments	http://www.lscog.org/
SC	Transit	Clemson Area Transit	http://www.catbus.com/
SC	Transit	Pee Dee Regional Transportation Agency	http://www.pdrta.org/
SC	Transit	Santee Wateree Regional Transit Authority	http://www.swrta.com/
SC	Transit	TriCounty Link	http://www.ridetricountylink.com/
WA	RPO	Yakima Valley Conference of Governments	http://www.yvcog.org/
WA	Transit	Mason County Transit	http://www.masontransit.org
WA	Transit	People for People	http://www.pfp.org/

www.ingramcontent.com/pod-product-compliance
Lightning Source LLC
Chambersburg PA
CBHW080343290526
45791CB00009BA/2713